HEALTH HEROES

EMILY SHARRATT

ILLUSTRATED BY JUANITA LONDOÑO

SIMON & SCHUSTER

First published in Great Britain in 2020 by Simon & Schuster UK Ltd

1 3 5 7 9 10 8 6 4 2

Simon & Schuster UK Ltd
1st Floor, 222 Gray's Inn Road
London
WC1X 8HB

www.simonandschuster.co.uk
www.simonandschuster.com.au
www.simonandschuster.co.in

Simon & Schuster Australia, Sydney
Simon & Schuster India, New Delhi

£1 from the sale of this book will be donated to NHS Charities Together,
a registered charity in England & Wales (no. 1186569)

A CIP catalogue record for this book is available from the British Library.

PB ISBN 978-1-4711-9721-5
PB export ISBN 978-1-4711-9783-3
eBook ISBN 978-1-4711-9720-8

Some names and identifying details have been changed to protect the
privacy of individuals.

Guardians of the young carers featured in this book have granted
permission for their extracts to appear in print and electronic publication.

Printed and bound by CPI Group (UK) Ltd, Croydon, CR0 4YY

MIX
Paper from
responsible sources
FSC® C020471

For Issy – my baby sister and my hero

THESE ARE THE HANDS

by Michael Rosen

These are the hands
That touch us first
Feel your head
Find the pulse
And make your bed.

These are the hands
That tap your back
Test the skin
Hold your arm
Wheel the bin
Change the bulb
Fix the drip
Pour the jug
Replace your hip.

These are the hands
That fill the bath
Mop the floor

Flick the switch
Soothe the sore
Burn the swabs
Give us a jab
Throw out sharps
Design the lab.

And these are the hands
That stop the leaks
Empty the pan
Wipe the pipes
Carry the can
Clamp the veins
Make the cast
Log the dose
And touch us last.

CONTENTS

WELCOME!

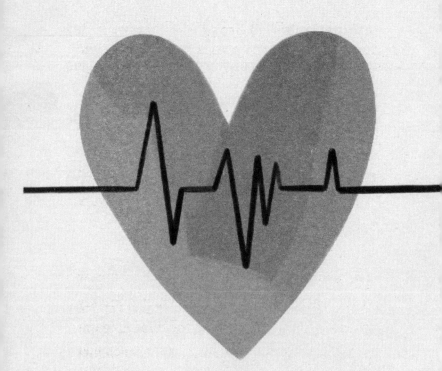

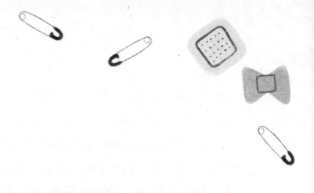

Welcome to this celebration of health heroes from all around the world!

You've probably needed to visit a doctor or nurse, or take a trip to a hospital at some point in your life, so you know that the people who work in healthcare – who look after us when we're unwell or injured – are important. But something happened at the very end of 2019 that really made the world stand up and take notice of these very special heroes.

That something was the outbreak of a new virus named COVID-19, which quickly spread around the world, becoming what is known as a pandemic. Governments everywhere shut down non-essential activity to try to slow the spread of the disease. Across the globe, people kept to their homes, seeing no one but the other members of their households, going outside only if they absolutely had to.

At the same time, doctors, nurses, midwives, paramedics, cleaners, cooks, porters, office staff and many others were working harder than ever, for longer hours, wearing uncomfortable protective clothing, in hospitals that quickly filled with sick patients – putting themselves at risk so the rest of us could be safe. Suddenly we couldn't miss the fact that these health heroes are all around us. And in fact, throughout history, whenever there has been sickness, pain, injury, hunger or sadness, we have never had to look far to find people working to make it better.

In this book, you will meet many health heroes from across time and around the world. But, of course, this is only the tiniest fraction of the total number of them.

A lot of the health workers you will meet in these pages are not sure about being called heroes. Some say they're just doing their jobs, or that they feel lucky in their work, or that they're normal people like the rest of us who simply want to earn a living and be safe at the same time.

But even as COVID-19 has spread worldwide, so too has something much more positive: people everywhere have begun to stand outside their homes, on balconies and doorsteps to clap and cheer and sing; to light up buildings, draw rainbows, and send messages, meals and love to the healthcare workers. To say, 'You might not feel like heroes, or even have chosen to be heroes, but we see your work and we won't ever forget it.'

So let's hear it for all the health heroes, past, present and future. Maybe you'll even grow up to be one of them!

As you read through, look out for words in **bold** – these words will be explained in more detail at the end of each section!

HEALTH HEROES THROUGH TIME

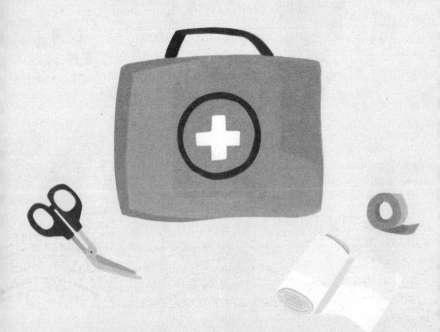

Health heroes have been around pretty much since humans have: for as long as we've existed we have needed the support of others when things haven't been working quite right with our bodies, when we've come into the world and when we've left it.

Medicine and healthcare haven't always looked like they do today, but early health heroes paved the way for the ones that followed. Across time, there have been too many health heroes to name them all, but here are a few . . .

Let's journey back...

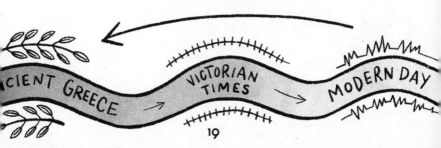

ANCIENT GREECE → VICTORIAN TIMES → MODERN DAY

ANCIENT GREEK HEROES

Many Ancient Greeks believed that illness was a punishment sent by the gods. But some of the cleverest people at the time were busy studying and exploring the natural world and the human body to find out how it all worked.

HIPPOCRATES
(around 460 BCE)

Very little is known about Hippocrates – including whether the work usually associated with him was done by one person or a group of people! – but he is thought to be one of the most important figures in the history of medicine. In fact, he is often referred to as the 'father of medicine'.

At a time when most people were very superstitious about sickness, he is believed to have taught that all illness had a natural cause. He wrote many documents on medicine, and gave his name to the Hippocratic Oath. This is still sworn by people today when they become doctors. In it they say they will always do their best and try never to do harm.

ARISTOTLE
(384–322 BCE)

Aristotle was fascinated with the world around him and how it worked. He thought you should not just believe something because of old ideas and superstitions, but that you should look and find out for yourself. This idea of having solid evidence for what you believe is still important in science and medicine today.

GALEN
(around 160 CE)

The son of a Greek architect and builder, Galen began his medical career taking care of gladiators in Turkey, before becoming **physician** to the emperors in Rome. Galen drew attention to the importance of understanding

WOW!!!

anatomy, the structure and function of the body. His studies on anatomy, diseases and drugs influenced western medical science for over a thousand years.

AGNODIKE
(around fourth century BCE)

Another Greek legend that may or may not be true tells of this Athenian woman who disguised herself as a man so that she could study medicine, which was against the law for women at the time.

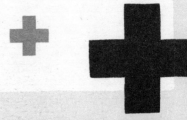

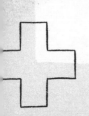

HEROIC WOMEN

It might seem strange now to think that for most of history, women were not allowed to study or work on the things that interested them or that they were good at, because it was believed they weren't capable of roles outside the home. In many parts of the world, things have changed a lot! Here are just a few of the women who were brave and determined enough to open a door for the ones who were to follow.

LADY MARY WORTLEY MONTAGU
(1689–1762)

This Englishwoman was famous for her letter writing. In one of her letters she described something called inoculation – where a small dose of a disease is introduced to the body to create immunity – which she had witnessed while living in Turkey.

At the time, a serious disease called smallpox affected many people all over the world. Lady Mary had lost her brother to smallpox, and she had suffered from it herself. To protect her son, she had him inoculated against the disease, making him perhaps the first English person to have this done. When she returned to England, she campaigned for inoculation to be made more widespread, though there was a lot of resistance to this idea at the time as it seemed so new, strange and risky.

In 1796, an English doctor named Edward Jenner developed a safer way of inoculating people against smallpox. He used what he called a vaccine, from a disease that was similar to smallpox, but not as deadly. Smallpox has since become the only disease to be completely wiped out thanks to widespread **vaccination**.

CUBAH CORNWALLIS
(late-1700s–1848)

Cubah was a Jamaican 'doctoress' or nurse who was so well known for her skills with traditional remedies that she was asked to tend both Horatio Nelson and Prince William Henry (later William IV). 'Cornwallis' was the name of the naval captain who had owned her as a slave, but she gained her freedom, and after Admiral Cornwallis left Jamaica, she went on to buy her own house, which she used as a small hospital.

Word got around!

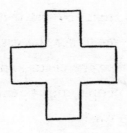

MARY SEACOLE
(1805–1881)

Mary was also from Jamaica. She showed an interest in caring for the sick from a very young age, helping her mother run a boarding house for ill and injured soldiers. She travelled a lot, working in the Caribbean and Central America before paying her own way to Europe to care for soldiers during the Crimean War (1853–56). There she set up what she called the 'British Hotel' near the battlefields, a place for the injured to receive food, rest and care. She earned such a reputation for her care that many of the soldiers called her 'Mother Seacole'. She even rode on horseback onto the battlefields to treat soldiers from both sides. Part of the secret of her success was that she kept everything very clean and hygienic at a time when people didn't realize how important this was.

FLORENCE NIGHTINGALE
(1820–1910)

Florence Nightingale is often considered the founder of modern nursing. During the Crimean War she tended to wounded soldiers, becoming known as 'the lady of the lamp' as she carried out rounds checking on her patients at night. But it was after the war that she did perhaps the most for the future of nursing, setting up the first professional nursing school at St Thomas' hospital in London in 1860. She also did lots of important work to improve healthcare for everyone in Britain, for example, by sending so-called Nightingale nurses to **workhouses**, so that the ill people living and working in them could be treated by trained professionals for the first time. She wrote a book called *Notes on Nursing* which introduced simple health rules for everyone to live by.

ELIZABETH GARRETT ANDERSON
(1836–1917)

Elizabeth was the first British woman to qualify as a doctor, despite having been rejected from every medical school she applied to. She signed up to study nursing and then sat medical exams at the Society of Apothecaries by finding a loophole in their rules.

Good thinking!

She continued to campaign for women's rights, and in 1876, women in Britain were finally officially allowed to qualify as doctors, though it wasn't until 1892 that the British Medical Association accepted female doctors.

MARY EDWARDS WALKER
(1832–1919)

Mary was the only woman in her class at medical school in New York in 1855. When she volunteered for the Union Army in the American Civil War she wasn't allowed to serve as a doctor at first. However, she later worked her way to being a surgeon in hospitals in Washington and later Ohio. After the war she campaigned for women's rights – including the right to dress comfortably and practically – and ran for political office – even though women weren't allowed to vote at the time!

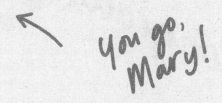
you go, Mary!

ANANDIBAI GOPALRAO JOSHI
(1865-1887)

Anandibai was the first female Indian doctor. She married very young and when her first baby died because she couldn't get him proper medical care, she decided she wanted to become a doctor. Her husband supported her, and when she was eighteen she went to America to study medicine. Queen Victoria heard of Anandibai and wrote to her to congratulate her for getting her medical degree.

Congratulations

CICELY WILLIAMS
(1893-1992)

Just after the First World War, Jamaican-born Cicely became one of the first women to earn a medical degree from Oxford university, going on to make huge advances in medicine for children and mothers, at a time when it was still very difficult to be a female doctor. She worked as a paediatric doctor all over the world, including Ghana, where she focused on children who were sick because of lack of food. During the Second World War, she was taken prisoner by Japanese forces, but was eventually released when the war ended. She later became the **World Health Organization**'s first head of **maternal** and child health.

HEROIC SURGEONS

For many, many years of human history, surgery was seen as being little more than butchery. In fact, early surgeons didn't have medical degrees and so couldn't be called 'doctor'. Even though you now can't become a surgeon without being a doctor, that funny quirk of history has remained, and once modern doctors pass their exams to become a surgeon they usually go back to being a 'mr', 'mrs', 'ms' or 'miss'!

Early surgery was painful, dangerous and often deadly, as there seemed to be no way for a surgeon to numb the patient's sensation or stop bleeding or infection. Because of this, surgery was usually a last resort,

Ouch!

when everything else had been tried – and had failed.

Things are different now, of course: surgeons are known for having to be exceptionally skilled and disciplined, and anaesthesia (a way of numbing pain), antibiotics and pain control have transformed surgery. Here are some of the great surgical pioneers that helped to move things forward.

AMBROISE PARÉ
(1510-1590)

A Frenchman, Ambroise focused on
relieving pain and on healing. He got rid of
the practice of cauterization
(burning the wound) to
stop bleeding, instead using
dressings and ligatures (a
way of tying up a wound
or a bleeding artery). These
were important steps towards
patients making a good
recovery from surgery.

Yikes!

JAMES BARRY
(1789–1865)

James travelled the world as a surgeon in the British Army, rising to the second highest rank. He campaigned everywhere to make hospitals and houses safer for people. He also learned how to do a safer **caesarean** (a surgery done for risky births), saving the mother's and baby's lives. James was called a girl when he was born, but lived all his adult life as a man. He became a doctor when gender rebels lived secretly, and when women weren't allowed to be doctors, so he's a hero for many people.

WILLIAM THOMAS GREEN MORTON
(1819–1868)

William was an American dentist who demonstrated the use of something called ether as a surgical **anaesthetic** – a substance that makes the patient sleepy and numbs pain – to a group of doctors in Boston. Many people had been trying to develop a general anaesthetic, so this was a big advance. It  enabled surgeons to carry out important operations without the patient feeling pain.

Only one year later, chloroform was successfully tried, and it quickly replaced ether as the preferred anaesthetic.

CHRISTIAAN BARNARD
(1922–2001)

In 1967 this South African surgeon carried out the first successful human heart **transplant**. This was a very risky operation, but the patient came round and his new heart worked on its own. Although he sadly died eighteen days later of pneumonia, surgeons worked hard to improve this life-saving treatment and now thousands of heart transplants are done across the world every year. Today, scientists continue to research ways to improve the long-term outcome for transplant recipients.

HEROIC DISCOVERIES AND INVENTIONS

The best ideas can come from the most unlikely places! Many curious minds – from doctors to painters to mathematicians – have made discoveries that have changed healthcare for ever. Here are a few examples.

LEONARDO DA VINCI
(1452–1519)

As well as his famous paintings, this Italian artist did many detailed drawings of the human body. These were based on his studies of corpses that he dissected – by the end of his life he claimed to have cut up more than thirty!

His discoveries and observations included making the first accurate drawing of the spine, and the structure and actions of the human heart, but he did not get around to publishing them before he died. It was only centuries later that his drawings were rediscovered and recognized as being groundbreaking.

gruesome!

WILLIAM HARVEY
(1578–1657)

This English doctor who treated, among others, King James I, was the first person to correctly describe how the heart works to pump blood around the body. This was key to understanding how the human body functions and some of the things that can go wrong with it, but it was only about twenty years later that his theory was widely accepted as correct.

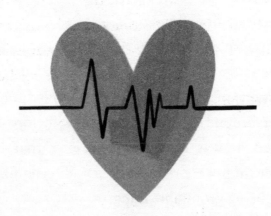

ANTONIE VAN LEEUWENHOEK
(1632–1723)

Antonie's job in Delft, Holland, was selling cloth. He found a way to make tiny but powerful lenses to look closely at the quality of the threads in material. He then realized he could use his microscope to look at other things. He was the first person to see and describe **bacteria**, which he called 'animalcules'. He also gave the first accurate definition of red blood cells. Both of these discoveries had a huge impact on medical research and development.

Aha!

RENÉ LAËNNEC
(1781–1826)

This Frenchman invented a simple stethoscope in 1816 – an instrument used to listen to the inside of the body that is still a symbol of doctors around the world today! A musician as well as a doctor, René was inspired in his design by the process of carving his own wooden flutes.

Take a deep breath in!

WILHELM RÖNTGEN
(1845–1923)

In 1895, this German physicist discovered X-rays, paving the way for doctors to see inside the human body without having to perform surgery. X-rays are a crucial part of medical practice today.

ALEXANDER FLEMING
(1881–1955)

In 1928 Alexander, a Scottish scientist, noticed the effects of mould on limiting the growth of bacteria. This led to his discovery of penicillin, a product of the mould. Penicillin is an important antibiotic, able to kill many of the bacteria that commonly infect humans. It has saved millions of lives.

MARIE CURIE
(1867–1934)

In 1898, three years after William Röntgen's discovery, the Polish-French scientist Marie Curie and her husband, Pierre, discovered a radioactive element that they called radium. It is still used in some types of cancer treatment today. During the First World War, Marie developed mobile X-ray units to help diagnose injuries near the front line. She went on to do more groundbreaking research into the treatment of cancer, and later her name was given to an organization that provides nursing care to people with terminal illnesses.

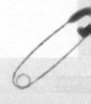

ATUL GAWANDE
(born 1965)

This American surgeon, writer and researcher was inspired by the simple but brilliant idea of another doctor called Peter Pronovost to use checklists when treating patients, as well as by the lists that pilots use when flying complex aircraft, to make sure they don't miss a crucial step.

Atul developed his own nineteen-point list for surgeons to use when operating. This was to make sure nothing gets forgotten, helping to reduce the potential for mistakes in very complicated procedures. The list includes important medical checks such as whether the patient has any allergies, or when they last had medicine, but also very simple things such as whether they've confirmed who they are, and if the part of the body to be operated on has been clearly marked! The **World Health Organization** took his recommendations on board and began to encourage surgeons around the world to use the checklist. Many countries have now signed up, and the hospitals that use it report a reduction in surgical complications, which means many lives have been saved.

Like a to-do List!

HEROIC GERM-BUSTERS

Nowadays we all know that washing our hands well and regularly is a very important and simple way of keeping healthy, as it helps to kill the germs that we all come into contact with every day and prevent them from entering our body. But believe it or not, this was not always the case!

IGNAZ SEMMELWEIS
(1818–1865)

Ignaz was a Hungarian doctor and scientist who discovered that good hand washing = less infection = fewer deaths! His discovery came about because he noticed in the

Vienna hospital where he worked that women whose babies were delivered on the midwives' ward developed a fever far less often than those who delivered their babies on the teaching ward, where they were examined by doctors and students. The difference? The midwives worked only in the labour ward, while the doctors and medical students also worked with dead bodies as part of their training. They weren't washing their hands afterwards, so they were transmitting infection from the corpses to the new mothers.

Wash your hands!

Unfortunately, because germs were not understood at the time, Ignaz's findings were not accepted by the medical community, many of whom were insulted at the suggestion that their hands were not clean!

LOUIS PASTEUR
(1822–1895)

This French scientist proved the connection between germs and disease. Pasteur had noticed that it was tiny **organisms** called bacteria that turned milk and wine sour and made food rot. He used these observations to explain that germs don't just come from nowhere, as had previously been believed – they are actual living things! His work was crucial to the understanding of germ theory, the idea that disease was caused by germs, and the functioning of the **immune system**. He did groundbreaking work on the development of vaccines to prevent some of the diseases that were such a big part of life and seemed unavoidable at the time.

HERMANN KÜMMELL
(1852–1937)

Towards the end of the nineteenth century, this German surgeon devised the process of 'scrubbing up', which medics still use now to ensure they are not exposing patients to bacteria while treating them. This simple action is now used around the world and helps to keep patients safe from infection.

DEFINITIONS

ANAESTHETIC: a kind of medicine that numbs pain

ANATOMY: the body or the study of the body

BACTERIA: small living things made from a single cell. Some cause disease

CAESAREAN: surgery to deliver a baby by cutting through the wall of the mother's abdomen

CIRCULATION: the movement of blood around the body, pumped by the heart

IMMUNE SYSTEM: the system in the body that fights off illness

IMMUNITY: the ability of a living being to resist a particular infection

INOCULATION: introducing a small amount of a disease into the body to create immunity

MATERNAL: relating to a mother, particularly during pregnancy and around childbirth

NERVOUS SYSTEM: the network – made up of brain, spine and nerves – that allows different parts of the body to communicate with each other

PAEDIATRICS: the branch of medicine relating to children

PHYSICIAN: a person qualified to practise medicine

TRANSPLANT: moving an organ or tissue of the body from one place or person to another

WORKHOUSES: in the past, in the UK, places where poor people could live and receive food in return for them working

WORLD HEALTH ORGANIZATION (WHO): an agency of the United Nations (UN) responsible for public health around the world

MODERN-DAY
HEALTH
HEROES

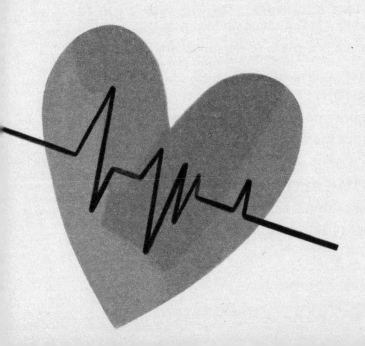

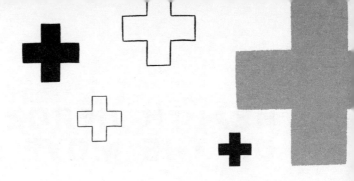

Health heroes throughout history came from all different places and backgrounds and did all sorts of healthcare jobs – and the same is true today. Now we're going to take you on a journey around some of the places you might find them, starting with a trip to the hospital.

HEALTH HEROES ON THE MOVE

Something has happened: perhaps you're not feeling well or you've had an accident and you have to go to hospital. Often we make our own way there, either for an appointment or if we've had a minor accident, but sometimes hospital transport – such as an ambulance, air ambulance (helicopter or plane) or even boat – with a specialist crew has to be sent to bring us in.

The crew aboard an ambulance varies from situation to situation, but can include:

* A *DRIVER* – ambulance drivers may or may not be qualified to provide medical care; sometimes they are needed to help transfer the patient, for example by stretcher

* A *FIRST RESPONDER* who can provide early critical care, such as **resuscitation** – these do not require medical training beyond first aid

* An *EMERGENCY TECHNICIAN* or *AMBULANCE TECHNICIAN* – these are usually trained in a range of emergency care skills, including resuscitation, controlling bleeding, giving medicines and providing oxygen

62

* A *PARAMEDIC* who has training to provide more advanced medical assistance, such as putting a **cannula** into a vein to deliver medicine, and **intubation**

* A *REGISTERED NURSE* – who sometimes attends instead of a paramedic, to provide highly skilled care

* A *DOCTOR*

Here's what some of the heroes who work in these fast-paced jobs have to say about their experiences.

JAMIE MILES

Jamie is a paramedic working in Yorkshire, England. It was the combination of 'a degree of thrill and excitement with my enthusiasm for science' that made him want to do the job. Jamie says:

'I LOVE attending patients where you can make a DIFFERENCE.'

One example of this was when he saved a newborn baby's life. 'I was working on a solo car [on his own as opposed to with team-mates] and got called to a woman who had given birth, and the baby wasn't breathing. I treated the baby by taking over her breathing and it worked! She started to pink up (colour came back into her skin) and take small breaths.'

Paramedics become very familiar with the area they work in. 'Being a paramedic, your experiences are made in the community you serve. An old hand once told me that as they drive from job to job, past houses or streets they've previously attended, the memory of the cases never fades. I completely agree.'

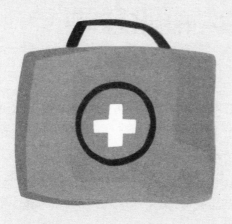

LUKE SUMMERS

Luke is in the process of becoming an emergency consultant, but he has worked as a retrieval registrar in Australia for many years. This means he has worked in helicopters,

'Flying around taking patients from where they get sick or injured to where the HELP is . . .

'This was a great opportunity to bring all my training together to look after patients by myself before I started work as a consultant. But more importantly I got to do it from the back of a helicopter flying all over the beautiful Queensland coast!'

Luke loved his helicopter work for a number of reasons. 'There is no better feeling than landing in a remote area where someone has been injured (especially if you have to **winch** in), then sorting them out and taking them to the hospital. You know they are probably having the worst time and by being there you get to make it bearable. Sometimes a patient will have something like a dislocated shoulder, or a bead stuck in their nose, or another fixable problem and you get to make it all better there and then. Plus, helicopters.'

It's not all dramatic rescues and stunning views – there are sad and scary moments in Luke's job too. 'Most of the worst stories that people have probably involve an emergency department. It's where you try to stop people from dying from things that would otherwise kill them. We are not always successful despite our best efforts.'

But sometimes it really is just as cool as it sounds. 'I once winched someone who was really sick from a cruise ship whilst it was sailing through the Coral Sea. We had to winch on to the deck and then back up again with the patient – not one to forget in a hurry.

'I also did a couple of winches from a mountain which was really cool. Very different from working in a hospital.'

TAYLOR HARKNESS

Taylor worked as a paramedic in America for many years. He is also a yoga instructor, who teaches all over the world, and is now working as an emergency nurse in Atlanta, Georgia. Taylor posted a picture of himself wearing his old paramedic uniform shirt on his Instagram account, with a caption explaining that he'd found it during a sort-out:

'A folded uniform shirt, still ringed with dirt and sweat around the collar. In the pockets were faded **EKG** strips, a couple of syringes, some long-since dried up alcohol prep pads and a pair of tattered gloves. The top was adorned with my badges of service – the only things I have ever kept from my past. [They] have seen more sweat, long sighs, blood, held-back tears, late-night delirious laughter with my partners and crews, tragedies, deaths, even a few births, unimaginable heaps of teamwork, total long shots and true miracles than I'll ever be able to recall.

'I decided to wash the uniform, try it on (still fits!) and hang it in the far corner of my closet – a reminder of why I went into this field in the first place, all those years ago: when things are dark and scary and heavy and full of gloom, the only real treasure we have is each other, and with that comes the responsibility to reach out, to help those in need, and do our own parts to the absolute best of our abilities. Those long nights on the ambulance put me through some of the most challenging experiences of my life, but

I would never trade the MEMORIES or the RELATIONSHIPS, and I would do it all again in a heartbeat.'

OLAMIDE OREKUNRIN

British-born Olamide was in the middle of her studies to become a doctor when her little sister fell ill while travelling with relatives in Nigeria. Olamide and her family were shocked to discover that there was no air ambulance service in the whole region, and tragically her sister died as they couldn't get her the care she needed. This terrible event made Olamide determined to create real change, and she went on to set up Flying Doctors Nigeria, the first air ambulance service in West Africa.

BRYNN BELL

Brynn has worked as a nurse in an outpatient office in New York for many years, but during the pandemic in April 2020, she was transferred to work with COVID-19 patients. 'Overnight I found out that I'd be getting training, and the next day I was on the floor working with patients.'

Within a couple of weeks she went from her normal office-based job to the ward, to then looking after patients on journeys within and outside hospital. 'COVID-19 patients need their oxygen levels to be monitored constantly, especially during transport when they are not able to have family or friends with them and might feel more nervous. The people doing the transport aren't medically trained, so my role has developed in these pandemic times. I get a report every day to say how many lives have been saved through this job.'

It's difficult work. 'Many patients are anxious; they're scared because they can't breathe.

'You have to be a CALMING influence. I try to SMILE and speak words of encouragement to them.

'I have met so many interesting people along the way, and made connections I never would have expected to make before. And humour is very healing – we try to laugh as much as possible. There's one transporter I work with who could be a comedian; he does a great Shrek impression!'

DEFINITIONS

CANNULA: a thin tube inserted into the body to administer medicine, drain fluid or introduce a surgical instrument

EKG OR ECG: a machine for measuring electrical signals from the heart, which it prints on strips of paper

INTUBATION: the insertion of a thin tube into the body, particularly for ventilation (help with breathing)

RESUSCITATION: reviving someone from unconsciousness

WINCH: using a device to lift someone on to a helicopter

HEALTH HEROES AT THE HOSPITAL

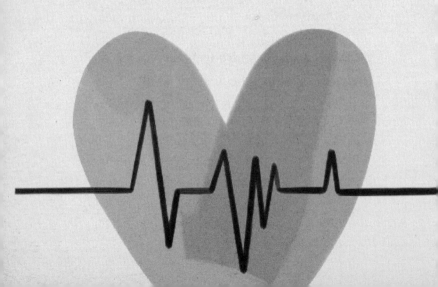

You've arrived at the hospital. Modern hospitals vary a lot depending on where you are, but within one, you might encounter some or all of the following heroes.

EMERGENCY AND INTENSIVE CARE HEROES

Perhaps the first health heroes that anyone thinks of – and those that most TV programmes and films focus on – are the ones who work in the hospital's **emergency department**, which can also be known as accident and emergency (A&E), the emergency room (ER) or casualty. As the names suggest, this is where you come if you need very urgent medical attention for whatever reason – and at any time. They often have their own special entrances, with easy access for ambulances.

HANNAH STEVENS

Hannah works as deputy **sister** in a children's accident and emergency (A&E) department in England. She decided she wanted to become a nurse because she was quite accident prone as a child and spent a lot of time in hospital with broken bones! She thought about training to become a paramedic, but 'my mum cried because she watched too many medical dramas on TV and she thought I was going to be killed in that job!' Of course, Jamie the paramedic could have reassured her that this isn't an occupational hazard he has to worry about!

Hannah knew she wanted to work in A&E after a work placement there in her second year of university. She loves the diversity of the patients. One of her favourite things about work is the thank-you cards she receives, which she feels make it all worthwhile. And some of her strangest and most memorable times have been on her many night shifts.

'Night shifts at about 4 a.m. are an odd time — EVERYTHING is hilarious!'

Sometimes, patients may be sent from an emergency department directly to an **intensive care unit (ICU)**, also known as an intensive therapy unit (ITU) or critical care unit (CCU). Patients also might be sent to one of these units after major surgery. ICUs are staffed by highly trained doctors, nurses and therapists, usually with more staff per patient than in other hospital departments. Patients here receive round-the-clock care and supervision, and usually need support from equipment that can monitor and medicate them as needed.

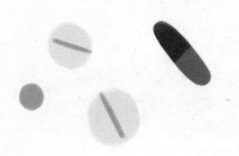

MATT MORGAN

Matt works in an intensive care unit in Cardiff, Wales. He also researches machinery and medicine for use in intensive care, and has written a book about his experiences. When he was at school, he told the careers adviser that he wanted to be an FBI agent, but growing up where he did in Wales, opportunities for this line of work were scarce! Now, though, he says every day in his job he uses science, encounters questions for which there are no answers, and his most valuable tool is the people he works with. So it doesn't feel that different from being a spy after all!

It's not always possible to save patients in intensive care, and that is very hard. 'But death is a part of life, and we have to be excellent at that aspect of care too. I take a lot of solace in making that part of a person's life as good as it possibly can be.' Matt isn't too keen on the 'more gory, gooey parts of the job. Blood? Okay. Poo? Just about all right. Snot and spit? No.' But there are funnier days at work. Once an entire rugby team came in after someone had played a practical joke on them by putting menthol rub into their food. 'We had to go around asking which of them was the greediest as they'd have eaten the most menthol!' Luckily they were all fine, but that's definitely not a trick to play on your friends!

Do not try this at home!

During the COVID-19 crisis in 2020, front-line medics had to wear special protective clothing, which made them hot and sweaty by the end of a long shift. Matt's favourite thing was walking through the corridor outside the unit to get some fresh air and seeing the walls lined with rainbows that children had drawn and sent in to say thank you to the keyworkers. 'That's the kind of thing that gets you through.'

For the most part, Matt feels lucky to have a job that he genuinely enjoys doing. He didn't find school easy and wouldn't have expected to end up with a career like this one.

'Often it's the choices you make in life rather than the abilities you have that make the difference. Be kind, work hard and ask questions. That's all you have to do.'

ABDULLAH BASHIR

Abdullah is also a doctor in intensive care
and in **respiratory** medicine – in London,
England – so his focus is on the lungs, and
on patients who are

'very, very sick.
In INTENSIVE CARE,
the patients are the
SICKEST people in
the hospital.'

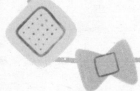

This, of course, means that it is not always possible to save lives. 'When people don't get better despite everything you've tried, when unfortunately people don't make it out of the ICU, that's the saddest and the hardest thing.' On the other hand, being able to help his patients, 'seeing them get well enough to leave our ward is a real joy'.

He decided to become a doctor aged eighteen. He says: 'I thought it would be a way to travel, a useful way to go all over the world – a romantic idea, with hindsight. And I wanted to have a practical skill. It's a handy thing, a cool skill to have, being a doctor. The hours are always a killer, but you get to meet people from all walks of life, both your colleagues and also patients, which is always fascinating. And jokes among staff members keep me going.'

CARLY MURDOCH

Carly is an ITU nurse and a senior sister for cardiac ITU in a central London hospital. She says she was prepared for how hard the job would be by her training: 'Nursing is not just a job, it's a vocation. Training was hard, I often had to work extra shifts to get some money, alongside the study and practical placements.'

Now, as a trained and experienced nurse, she says, 'The hardest thing is the sad situations that you face daily. The relatives and loved ones that never had that opportunity to say goodbye. But that leads me on to the best thing – being the nurse that cares for these patients in their final hours. It's a privilege to be given that opportunity to make it as nice as possible. I always, always hold my patients' hands as they take their last breaths, sit with them and just take time to allow them this moment at the very end of their lives. It's an honour to do that. I will never forget the name of my first patient that I cared for as she passed away.'

Carly says it is her colleagues that help her through incredibly sad moments like this, as well as the happier ones.

'The camaraderie, the TEAM SPIRIT, especially in ITU, is essential . . .

'Being able to share happy and sad moments with colleagues and friends who truly understand what you are feeling and going through. Only nurses truly understand nurses.'

Which isn't to say that they don't show that love for each other in funny ways! 'We do have a giggle because you absolutely have to. When one of the nurses left we covered him in shaving foam, squirted him with water and stuck all manner of stuff on him. He had a great time!'

SHELBY DELANEY

Shelby is an ICU nurse in a busy California hospital. During the COVID-19 crisis in April 2020, Shelby posted a photo on her Instagram account of her wearing the basketball jersey of her favourite player – Stephen Curry of the Golden State Warriors – under her protective gear. A caption explained that the jersey helped her to find her 'inner warrior' and empowered her to work through the incredibly challenging circumstances, and to find solutions to problems, such as campaigning for more life-saving protective equipment for her and her ICU colleagues.

Stephen Curry heard about Shelby and video-called her and her team-mates while she was on duty, to thank them for their work.

CHILDREN'S HEROES

A very different part of the hospital is the area where babies are born. This unit has lots of different names around the world, including **maternity**, antenatal or **obstetrics**. The people who work here help to bring new life into the world!

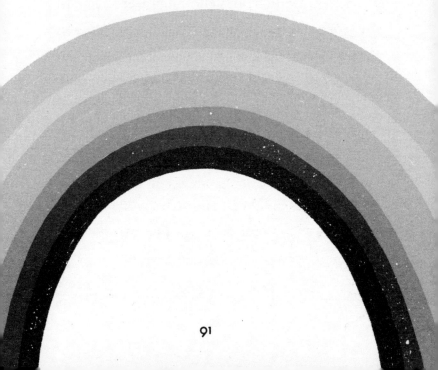

SARAH DRIVER

Sarah has two jobs: she works as a midwife in a hospital in the south of England, and she also writes books for children. So she's a hero twice over: she helps to bring new people into the world, and then she feeds their imaginations with stories.

Sarah trained as a nurse to begin with 'which is one route in, though much less common now', before going on to further training to become a midwife. Sarah loves the variety of her role as a midwife, but 'even better than that are the people, who really make it a joy – the families I work with and my funny, supportive, tough colleagues. Their warmth, humour and tenacity are second to none.'

Sarah's job might seem like a very happy one, but that's not always the case. 'The worst thing that's happened at work would be encountering death, at a time which is typically associated with joy. Midwives know this isn't always so. We have to be able to care for families in their darkest moments as well as their happiest. I hope kindness and care sometimes help, and that at least people's memories of how they were treated might go some small way towards easing the trauma.'

At the other extreme, there are funny moments too. 'Once, as a student, I was standing by a woman's bedside while she was in labour, and my mentor was at the foot of the bed. Suddenly, the **membranes** ruptured [the waters broke], evidently with a great deal of pressure behind them, and my mentor was drenched in a tidal wave of fluid, while I looked on from dry land.' Perhaps this story was part of the inspiration behind

Sarah's amazing fantasy adventure series, The Huntress, which features a midwife character aboard a ship!

Most of all, though, Sarah says:

'It's so HUMBLING to accompany families on such huge life journeys, and to receive their TRUST.
It is an HONOUR.'

SHIREEN HICKEY

Shireen works as an obstetric and **gynaecology** registrar (doctor) in Yorkshire, England. She says: 'Being present at the birth of a baby is a huge privilege and despite being present at thousands it has never lost its magic.'

Shireen wanted to become a doctor to follow in her grandad's footsteps but, 'I didn't get the grades I needed to get into medical school the first time around,' she says, 'so I had to do another degree first. But when you really want something, don't give up, you'll get there in the end! It took me fourteen years of school and eight years of university. But it was worth every single day.'

Shireen says that sometimes sad things happen at work,

'but this is where TEAMWORK is so important. We all SUPPORT each other through the hard times so that we can be there for the good times too.'

Good times like when the consultant on Shireen's ward dressed up as Father Christmas and delivered presents to all the babies born on Christmas Day!

Once you're older than a newborn baby, up until you're sixteen (or eighteen, or even twenty-one in some parts of the world), the part of the hospital you're most likely to be sent to is **paediatrics**.

ALEXA CANADY

Alexa began by studying maths at university, and nearly dropped out of the course due to a lack of confidence – but she went on to become the first female African-American **neurosurgeon** in the USA. Her focus was on paediatric neurosurgery, and she saved the lives of thousands of children and young people. Despite being a brilliant student and doctor, Alexa faced a lot of prejudice, particularly early in her career, and she had to work harder than anyone to overcome this. But she became known all over America for her great work, winning many awards and honours.

ISSY SHARRATT

Issy is a paediatric nurse specialist in **endocrinology** (focusing on the different glands, and the **hormones** they release) in a London hospital. She has wanted to work in paediatrics ever since meeting the amazing **neonatal** nurses when her little brother was born three and a half months early.

'I KNEW about paediatrics almost BEFORE I understood what nursing was!'

Straight after qualifying, Issy worked in a paediatric intensive care unit, looking after very poorly child patients and working long shifts, including overnight. She says her favourite part of that job was 'de-intensifying' a patient when they began to get better: 'basically removing all the tubes and wires they have been relying on but don't need any more. That was very satisfying. It was lovely to give them to a parent or carer to cuddle for the first time in days or weeks.'

Her job now in endocrinology is very different: 'It's lovely that we rarely have **inpatients**. I love sending patients home at the end of the day!'

Issy's favourite part of the job is the funny things some of her patients say. One little boy who received growth hormone treatment came in for a check-up. When he was being weighed, he announced, 'I'm a big boy now because you're giving me a magic potion to grow!'

REBECCA CRESPI

Rebecca is another paediatric nurse specializing in endocrinology, but she's in a different busy city – New York! She also teaches children and their families about **diabetes**, and how to live with it. Diabetes is a disease that affects how the body deals with **glucose** – the sugar that our bodies use as fuel.

'My FAVOURITE part of my job is the people I meet. I love HELPING PEOPLE and being able to make a difference in someone's life. Since diabetes is a lifelong condition, I get to see many of these children GROW UP and manage a chronic medical condition which can be frustrating but is also AMAZING!

'I love my team too. The nurses and doctors and dieticians that I work with are awesome! Caring for children is a team approach and we are all good at different parts of it. I also get to work with people outside of my office and direct team. **Pharmacists** and people who work at the **pharmaceutical** companies to make the medicines for my patients, and people who work in the companies that make medical equipment like **insulin** pumps. Mental health professionals (social workers and psychologists), and the receptionists. Everyone has the same goal – helping the patients succeed, be safe and be healthy! I feel very supported by those nurses who are in it with me. No one understands better than they do. All of the nurses and NPs (nurse practitioners) are ROCK STARS!'

MIA NOAH

Mia is English but used to live in New York, where she worked for the Make a Wish Foundation, a charity that makes wishes come true for critically ill children. There she met a health play specialist – someone who uses play techniques to help children understand and cope with their treatment and being in hospital – who told her she'd be perfect for the job.

She qualified and worked as a play specialist in Texas and Cambodia before moving back to England. Mia loves her job, especially when she's able to help 'a child to do something that they might have been put under general anaesthetic for otherwise. So guiding a child through an **MRI** or **radiotherapy**, for example.

'My job allows me to laugh a lot. I love playing every day and being the happier part of a child's treatment.'

RANJIT SINGH
- DR RANJ!

Known as 'Dr Ranj' Ranjit is a paediatric emergency doctor in London and other hospitals around the UK. He is also a TV presenter and writer, and was a celebrity dancer on *Strictly Come Dancing*, where he proved that he is a hero on the dancefloor as well as in the hospital! Among his other television work, Dr Ranj presents TV programmes on health for children. During the COVID-19 crisis in 2020, he continued to work at the medical front line and he also produced videos answering questions children had about the virus.

what a star!

HEROES IN THE OPERATING THEATRE

When you need an **operation** to either investigate or treat a medical condition, you are sent for surgery. Sometimes emergency operations are needed – at other times they are planned in advance. Surgery usually takes place in what is called an 'operating theatre' on an 'operating table', using specially designed instruments. Staff in an operating theatre must wear **sterile** clothing, and they must 'scrub up' – thoroughly wash their hands and arms – before entering the theatre and before each procedure, to minimize the spread of germs, which can put vulnerable patients even more at risk.

R. P. NARAYAN

Dr Narayan is a professor and consultant doctor specializing in burns, and **plastic** and **cosmetic surgery** in Delhi, India. Dr Narayan wanted to follow in the footsteps of his father, who was also a doctor.

'I have ALWAYS felt a commitment to do BETTER for the people here in this country . . .

'"To restore and reconstruct" is the motto of plastic surgery. My favourite part has been treating young children, restoring parts of the body which have been deformed since birth such as a **cleft lip palette**, or which have undergone trauma. The chance of giving a normal life for such children is deeply uplifting.'

JASON CAMPBELL – THE TIKTOK DOC!

Jason is an American anaesthetist who has become famous as the 'TikTok Doc' after he posted videos of himself and his colleagues dancing. 'Someone asked me why TikTok? Why the dancing videos? I told them in twenty years I want to see more women in surgery, Black men in medicine and female leaders. So, I had to meet the youngest generation where they're at . . . now we can have those discussions.' The dancing videos are a great way of getting their attention and letting them know that doctors are people just like them!

Dancing Doc

RADIOLOGY HEROES

If doctors want to use high-tech methods like **X-rays**, **MRI** or **ultrasound** to look inside you to find out, or treat, what's wrong, you will probably be sent to the radiology department – it's full of the cleverest gadgets! Meet some heroes who work in this important area.

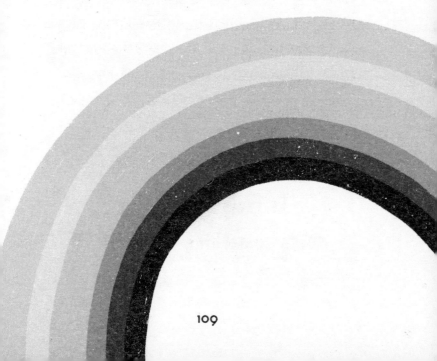

HANNAH WARNER

Hannah works as a radiologist in Vancouver, Canada. She decided to specialize in radiology after becoming a doctor because she 'liked finding out what the problems were inside patients, and I loved all the pictures!' Like some of the other health heroes we've met, Hannah finds it difficult when there isn't a clear answer to the question. 'Sometimes you really want things to work out for someone and they don't. Sometimes you only get the answer when things have already gone wrong.' But it means a lot to her when she knows she's made a difference to patients or their loved ones.

'It feels great to be doing something USEFUL.'

VICKI DOUGLAS

Vicki is a radiographer in a hospital in Dublin, Ireland. 'That means that I take X-rays of people's bones. They show things like breaks and **arthritis**. I always wanted to work in a hospital because I like caring for people. My job is great because I get to meet lots of people and I like working as part of a team. And every patient is unique.'

Vicki says that the nicest thing that has ever happened to her in work was 'a patient's parent sent me a lovely letter and a box of chocolates thanking me for taking care of their six-year-old daughter who had been afraid of getting an X-ray because the machine looked big and scary. I told her it was just a big special camera and it wouldn't hurt, and then I showed her the X-ray afterwards.'

There are lots of really cool moments. 'Once I X-rayed a little boy who had swallowed a coin. The X-ray helped to locate where it was so it could be removed.'

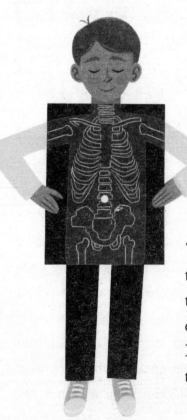

The most important thing Vicki wants to tell you is: 'If you ever have to have an X-ray, don't forget to say cheese!'

HEROES ALL OVER THE HOSPITAL

But as well as these more well-known parts of the hospital, there are many others – different departments for just about anything that can go wrong with a human body!

LORNA BEGG

Lorna is a **physiotherapist** in a brain injury unit in a hospital in Manchester, England. She helps people recover physically from the damage that can be done to the body by a brain injury. She was always interested in science and 'practical hobbies', and knew she wanted to do a job that made a real difference to people's lives, but she tried a few other career paths before she came to this one.

Lorna's job is often technically very challenging, and she says, 'it can also be very difficult accepting the fact that sometimes there is a limit to what a therapist can achieve towards patients' goals. Sometimes there is a ceiling of possible recovery, depending on how severe a patient's brain injury is.'

But on the other hand, she says she is very aware of 'the privilege of helping people to

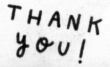

become more independent, by re-training them how to complete basic tasks, which can make a huge difference to their quality of life.

'Most of the time, we only spend approximately three months with our patients, on their rehab journey. Then we hand over the baton to teams in the community, who carry on working with patients towards their long-term goals. So, patients may not have reached their full potential while on our unit. One of my patients progressed so quickly, we were able to complete most of her journey together; from her being bed-bound, and unable to roll, to being able to walk independently.

'I will always keep her detailed card of THANKS, to remind me of what's possible.'

BECKY LANTZOS

Becky is a speech and language therapist in a New Zealand hospital. She works with patients who have difficulty with communication or swallowing – which of course means it can be difficult for them to eat and drink. Becky became fascinated by speech and language therapy when she had a placement on a **stroke** unit as part of her nursing training.

'When I think about swallowing ability, someone's ability to EAT and DRINK, and also EXPRESS themselves, I see those things as BASIC HUMAN RIGHTS – an essential part of life.'

Like so many health heroes, Becky thinks the people she meets and works with – whether patients or colleagues – are the best part of her job. She also loves being able to help a patient towards an outcome they really wanted and worked for. 'Being able to support someone towards a lifelong goal – for example, we've had someone before who's wanted to be able to make a speech at a family member's wedding, and that was really rewarding to support them towards that. Or if someone sets a target of being able to have a couple of teaspoons of a food that they really like – when they get there it's an amazing feeling, because you've been on that journey with them.'

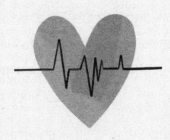

SUJITH SUBESINGHE

Sujith is a rheumatology consultant in a central London hospital. That means his focus is on diseases of the body's system of muscles and bones. 'Many of the conditions I treat are related to the immune system not working properly, resulting in the body "attacking" itself.'

The son of two doctors, Sujith grew up listening to their stories and always knew he wanted to follow the same path. 'As a consultant, it is a privilege to be able to lead the team caring for a patient. I enjoy the fact that I can have long-term care for patients too. This means I will be able to see their progress over several years and I can witness the impact of my treatments.'

Sujith says that this satisfaction has come at a cost, over his many years of training and work. 'I've missed birthdays, family gatherings and friends' weddings due to work. I've spent weekends, days and nights in the hospital. Work doesn't end when I leave the hospital. It can be very hard to detach.

'But the BEST part of my job is having the RESPONSIBILITY for HELPING PEOPLE when they are at their MOST VULNERABLE, and the trust that they place in me to get them back to HEALTH.'

BEHIND-THE-SCENES HEROES

When we think about health heroes, the people who immediately come to mind will probably be doctors, nurses and other front-line health workers. But there are all sorts of other heroes working away in a hospital, often out of sight, trying to make sure you are as comfortable, safe and well as you can possibly be during your time there. They are the heroes that help the hospitals to run smoothly and allow the medical professionals to do their jobs.

GILLIAN LEWIS

Gillian is head of what is called 'quality **governance**' in a London hospital. This very complicated job title means she is in charge of the safety of patients, making sure they are happy with their experience at the hospital, and keeping track of how well things are working within it.

'Like most people who work in health and social care, the best bit of my job is making a difference to patients' lives. Risk management is a large part of my job, which is about identifying problems before they happen to prevent future harm. If you do it right, no one sees it! On the flip side, ask any front-line worker and they will give you hundreds of ideas about how to improve care for their patients, but most don't have the time to put them into practice. Others don't know how to turn an idea into a practical plan. I get to help with that, which is great!

'One aspect of my job is about FIXING THE SYSTEM, not the people. People are human and will make mistakes — be tired, hungry, act instinctively. Part of my job is making the system SAFE so that when people have those bad days, they don't affect the patient.'

HASSAN AKKAD

Cleaning is a hugely important job within the hospital, to ensure that germs are not spread between sick people, or to vulnerable patients. Hassan Akkad is a Syrian filmmaker who came to the UK as a refugee, and has since campaigned for the rights of other refugees. During the 2020 COVID-19 crisis, Hassan volunteered at his local London hospital as a cleaner. After being trained, he said he was honoured to join a team of cleaners disinfecting COVID wards. Since coming to the UK, Hassan thinks of London as his home, and of this work as supporting his neighbours, and helping to keep NHS staff safe.

ASMA BEGUM

Nadiya Hussain won the *Great British Bake Off* competition in 2015 and has since become known as a TV chef and presenter, as well as a writer. During the coronavirus pandemic, she posted a picture of herself and her mum, Asma, on her Instagram account with a caption explaining that her mum works in a hospital, washing all the linen that gets used and dirtied over the course of the day. Nadiya pointed out that we might not think of her mum's job when we visit a hospital, but that we'd certainly be stuck without her and her colleagues. And she reminded us that we shouldn't forget their work when the pandemic is over!

ALPHA BARRY

Alpha is at university, but during his holidays, he works as a porter in a south London hospital. 'My dad's a cleaner at the same hospital. When I was going to uni, he was worried I'd get lazy, so to make sure I didn't, he told me to get a job at the hospital too!'

Alpha's job involves taking patients and equipment around the hospital. 'It can be quiet on weekdays, but at the weekends, on a Friday night in A&E, for example, you're usually rushed off your feet, running back and forth all shift. On a busy night you can do twenty transfers. It's a very physical job – a decent level of fitness is needed.' Mind you, that can be quite satisfying: 'You feel like you've really done a day's work!'

Alpha finds talking to the patients the most interesting part of the job.

'People usually want to TALK to you, and they can be really FUNNY or INTERESTING . . .

'One guy I spoke to used to work for MI5 and he had amazing stories. Another one had danced with the Royal Ballet and travelled all over the world.'

And of course both the hospital staff and the inpatients need to eat! Many hospitals have whole teams in charge of providing meals and refreshment for all the patients, staff and visitors.

HELEN WILSON

Helen usually works as a pilot, but during the 2020 COVID-19 crisis, when most flights were grounded, she joined a team of airline staff volunteering in London hospitals to provide 'tea and empathy, a place to relax and unload, for all the wonderful staff working on the front line'.

It's very different from her normal job.

'I'm not used to spending so much time on my feet — it gives me a NEW APPRECIATION for my cabin crew colleagues and the clinical staff at the hospital!

'It's humbling to be able to meet and in some small way thank some of the wonderful staff that are working on the front line. When I first started volunteering I wondered how much difference making someone a cup of tea would really make, whether it was a worthwhile thing to be doing. But there have been many moments that have shown me that it is. In our first week, we had a visit from several doctors from the paediatric ward, who had had a particularly hard night shift. We sat them down, made them hot drinks and listened to them. It didn't seem very much at the time, but each doctor individually came back to thank us for our support in the week following.'

DEFINITIONS

ANTENATAL: before birth

ARTHRITIS: a disease that causes inflammation and stiffness of the joints

CHRONIC: an illness that lasts a long time or comes back repeatedly

CLEFT PALETE: a split in the roof of the mouth that is present from birth

CONSULTANT: in the UK, a senior hospital doctor

COSMETIC SURGERY: an operation that is done to improve appearances rather than for medical reasons

ENDOCRINOLOGY: the branch of medicine that relates to glands and the hormones they release

GLANDS: organs in the body that give out certain chemical substances

GLUCOSE: a simple sugar that is an important energy source in living creatures

GOVERNANCE: the running of an organization (here, a hospital)

GYNAECOLOGY: the branch of medicine that relates to women's bodies, specifically the female reproductive system

HORMONES: substances the body produces to trigger certain cells or tissue into action

INPATIENT: a patient who lives in hospital while undergoing treatment

INSULIN: a hormone produced in the pancreas, which controls the amount of glucose in the blood

MEMBRANES: a thin sheet of tissue or cells (here, the sac of amniotic fluid)

MIDWIFE: a person trained to assist women in childbirth

MRI: (short for magnetic resonance imaging) a way of creating images of the inside of the body using radio waves and magnetic fields

NEONATAL: this literally means 'newborn', but as a branch of medicine refers to the care and treatment of babies born prematurely and/or with health conditions

NEUROSURGEON: a surgeon focused on the nervous system, especially the brain and spinal cord

NHS: the free National Health Service in the UK

OBSTETRICS: the branch of medicine concerned with pregnancy and childbirth

PAEDIATRIC: the branch of medicine relating to children

PHARMACEUTICAL: relating to drugs used as medicine

PHARMACIST: a person who is qualified to prepare and give out medicines

PLASTIC SURGERY: reconstructing or repairing the body by moving tissue from one place to another

RADIOTHERAPY: the treatment of disease using X-rays or other forms of radiation

REGISTRAR: in the UK, a middle-ranking hospital doctor who is being trained as a specialist

RESPIRATORY: relating to breathing or the lungs

RESIDENT: in the US, a doctor receiving specialist training while under supervision in a hospital

STERILE: free from microorganisms or germs

STROKE: a sudden interruption in the flow of blood to the brain

ULTRASOUND: sound waves that can be used to form a picture of the inside of the body

HEALTH HEROES IN THE COMMUNITY

Health heroes can be found outside the hospital too, helping us in our communities, at doctors' surgeries, pharmacies, care homes, hospices – even visiting us in our own homes.

LOCAL PRACTICE HEROES

For many of us, the health heroes we encounter most often are in our local doctors' surgeries – GPs (general practitioners), nurses, healthcare assistants and receptionists.

MOHAN SEKERAM

Mohan is a GP, or family doctor, in London, and he also trains new GPs. When he was studying to be a doctor he thought he would like to work in emergency medicine, as it seemed the most exciting. But during his training he really connected with family and community medicine. He values 'getting to spend time with a family over many years, decades, getting to know families and individuals, to form those relationships; see them through the ups and downs; offering consistent care'. He also appreciates the extra time he can spend with a patient in non-emergency situations, 'being able to use my knowledge as well as my experience; helping with a patient's health and well-being, with a bigger picture than you see in urgent care'.

Mohan also likes the social side of his work – the interaction with patients and other staff.

'The NHS is a nice family. I like the variety of my work too. You don't get the same day twice.'

Mohan thinks that a lot of people's first instinct is to go to the doctor for a quick cure, 'a magic pill', when they're not well. He helps people to see that there are other factors, such as stress, anxiety, dehydration, poor diet and so on, which can have a much bigger impact. His motto is: 'A balanced approach to life is the best medicine you can have.'

AILEEN HICKEY

Aileen is a GP too, in a different part of London. She says that the

'hardest part of my job is breaking BAD NEWS to patients, but this can still be rewarding if you feel you have done it well.

'I don't see myself as a fixer or a curer but as a listener and investigator. There are many physical conditions that I see on a day-to-day basis that are easily fixed, and it's rewarding to do so, but most of my job involves asking questions (that most people don't get to ask – lucky me!) in order to get to know people and their background.'

Like Mohan, she loves the relationships she can build with her patients working as a GP.

'I have now been at the same surgery for long enough to get to know entire families and can use the information I have about this dynamic and background to better care for my patients. As a general practitioner, I get to learn about and look after babies, children, teenagers, adults, the elderly and am lucky enough to care for patients in the final stages of their life, which is such an intimate time for families – I feel very privileged to be part of this. I get to learn about all the different conditions that can affect us from cradle to grave, which means my breadth of knowledge has to remain vast!'

This interest in people's lives was what led Aileen to want to be a doctor. 'I am very nosy by nature, and I love finding out about people. As a child, I would choose sitting in the kitchen with my mum, listening to her talk (gossip!) with her friends and family about people they knew, over playing outside with other children. I was and still am fascinated by real lives, real people, real stories and real problems.

'The other massive contributing factor to my decision to do medicine was my grandad, who was a GP in the town I grew up in. I was in complete awe of him and loved that he could make my earache and sore throat better – even without doing anything, just having him look in my throat and ears was instantly soothing. I thought that he was magic, and I wanted to do what he could do one day! He was very well known and much admired in our town, and I was so proud of him. I loved it when people realized I was his granddaughter and thought I had an extra special grandad compared to all my friends.'

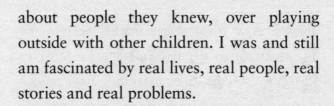

Open wide!

HOSPICE AND CARE HOME HEROES

Hospices and care homes are places that provide somewhere for people to live and receive treatment or care when they are very unwell at the end of their lives, or old and unable to look after themselves. Meet some of the heroes who do this important work.

SARAH DOWD

Sarah is a social worker in a hospice – somewhere that provides care for people at the end of their lives. 'Sometimes people are sad, unwell or facing challenges and they

need someone to help them get their voice heard.' Sarah's job is to support them in this.

'My favourite part of the job is meeting new people every day!

'I feel very privileged that people SHARE their STORIES with me and I can hopefully be part of making their lives BETTER in some way.

'Sometimes it can be sad. I work with people when they have illnesses which they will one day die from. Lots of the time my job is about supporting people to live their lives right up until they die.

'Being a social worker can be hard, but it can also be a job in which we witness people use their own skills and beliefs to completely transform their lives, which is wonderful!'

BARBARA GEORGE

Barbara works in a hospice too, but she is in charge of running the IT side of things: collecting and organizing data and keeping records, as well as training staff on using the hospice's computer systems.

'The BEST thing is that though you move around, you gain LIFELONG FRIENDS. Your work family is very important.'

She also likes learning new skills (embracing her 'inner geek'), and finding practical solutions to problems.

Barbara used to be a medical secretary and really liked the contact with patients in that role. It was after her own mum died that she decided to work in a hospice.

'So much of that was about trying to TRANSLATE for the family when they didn't UNDERSTAND why things couldn't be different. After that I realized how HARD it is on the outside with no medical knowledge.'

Working in a role like hers seemed like a good way to be a bridge between patients and the families on one side, and the medics on the other.

NURSING HEROES

ROMA BISSESSAR

Roma is retired now, but she was a community nurse for many years, which means she worked outside of hospitals, treating and caring for patients in local clinics and health centres. Roma came over to the UK from Trinidad to train as a nurse when she was just eighteen, having never spent a night away from home before then. 'I was very homesick, especially when the summer came.' Roma had left school at sixteen and joined the British Red Cross Society, then the ambulance brigade. Roma found it impossible to get into nursing training in Trinidad as it was many people's first choice of work when they left school, so she had to move all the way to England, where there was a greater need for nurses.

When she first qualified, Roma worked in a **psychiatric** ward, then as a general nurse, both of which were very challenging, and it was in community nursing that she had 'the happiest time ever'. She loved getting to know the other staff and working as a team. Roma says the best moment of her career was when one day she realized she could take blood, understand test results, do **CPR** and **catheterization**, and help doctors with other investigations.

'That's when I KNEW I was a responsible nurse.'

NICOLA STONE

Nicola worked as an intensive care nurse for many years, but now her job is 'all about enabling people who haven't been able to access nurse training (due to finances or dependents or other life events) to become nurses. It means that these people, who have the great qualities that we look for in nurses, can actually nurse patients. I love watching nurses I've taught and supported develop and thrive and enjoy their work.'

Nicola says, 'nurses are often talked about as heroes or angels – and that's a long way from what nursing is about and who nurses are. Nurses are educated, intelligent, thoughtful, analytical, talented people who are internally driven to care for others. The feeling when you've made a difference is unbeatable. People think it is a hard job; it is, but it's also one of the most rewarding for sure!'

MENTAL HEALTH HEROES

Just as important as our physical health is our mental health, and there are many heroes whose work focuses on just that.

MAGGIE MAY

Maggie is training to become a **clinical psychologist**. This means she 'works with people to help them make sense of their feelings or experiences. We then think together about the best way of supporting them to make things better in their lives, and we do this through talking. But if people don't like to talk much, that's okay too, we

can also use drawing, play and diagrams to help people communicate.

'I love hearing about people's lives and their stories, getting to know them and ultimately help them to feel better and be the best version of themselves (and this is something they do for themselves. I can't take credit for that!).

'Sometimes people tell me about things that have HURT or SCARED them, but there is LAUGHTER too . . .

'Once I was at the house of a lady who was feeling really sad. She had a wild cat as a pet and I'm not very good with cats – they scare me a bit. This cat was very big! I think he knew I was a little scared and decided to chase me around the sofa, paw at my feet and then wee on me. I couldn't stop laughing (or running around the sofa). The lady who I was seeing found this hilarious and laughed like I'd never heard her laugh before. It was a really funny and nice moment and in a weird way helped us make our relationship stronger because we had laughed together so much.'

A warm Welcome!

HEROES IN YOUR HOME

You might even find some health heroes in your own home!

KATHERINE DRYDEN

Katherine is retired now but worked as a head of nursing for children's services. She is really proud of the service for children with complex and long-term needs that she set up in the community. This service brought together a team of paediatric nurses and healthcare assistants to work with children and their families in their own homes. It was designed 'to support families to enable the children to stay at home, get early discharge from hospital and attend school. It was a challenging job, which I loved. The team was built up over time with fantastic, committed staff.'

One mum said that this support enabled her and others to be

'the parents we want to be'.

In her forty years of working, Katherine had too many stories to choose from, but she remembers a funny occasion when she was working as the on-call manager and took 'a call from a community hospital ward sister telling me there was a fox on the ward and asking what should she do!'

SALLY KILNER

Sally is a health visitor, working with families that have preschool children. 'I decided to go in to health visiting as I wanted to be able to support families at a community level, to be able to work with them for a sustained period of time to help them make positive changes, and help children to do well and achieve their potential. I think childhood is such a massively important time. It can shape our futures and adulthood.

'My favourite part of my job is visiting new mums and babies. I know from having my own baby that it can be a time of mixed emotions, and I was not prepared at all for how I would feel. I visited a mum recently who was tearful, finding breastfeeding really challenging and was not leaving the house. I spent lots of time exploring her feelings about feeding and what she wanted to do. When I visited the week after she was looking so much better in herself. She said the advice I had given her had changed her life. It felt so rewarding knowing that just some simple advice and support had made such a big difference, not only to her special time with her new baby, but also for her emotional health and well-being too. There have been quite a few funny moments at work with babies weeing on the scales (when they're being weighed) and I have seen my colleagues jumping out of the way in baby clinics. I have only been weed on once, which I think is quite lucky.'

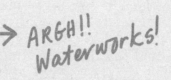

ARGH!!
Waterworks!

ANNA FAIRLEY

Anna is a midwife, but rather than working in the hospital, her job is to support people who choose to have their babies at home. Anna really enjoys the cosiness of home births: 'I love making new mummies tea and toast after they have just given birth, it feels like the simplest yet most deserved treat I can provide after all the hard work.' A real highlight was 'delivering the baby of my dear friend, who is also a midwife'.

There can be stresses that hospital midwives don't usually have to deal with.

'The WORST thing that ever happened at work was getting lost on the way to a home birth and being scared that I was going to miss the baby arriving.'

But overall, it's a very rewarding job. 'My favourite part of being a midwife is seeing the transformation of women from pregnancy, during their birth and afterwards. There's something so special about looking after someone in their homes throughout pregnancy, before the baby is born, and then seeing them back at home with their new baby and helping them settle into their new role as a mum!'

There's another kind of health hero working not in other people's homes but in their own. These heroes aren't paid for their work – they do it out of love. They are carers or care-givers – usually family members who look after a child, sibling, parent, grandparent or friend. And among these carers is a very special group known as young carers – those aged eighteen and under, who help to look after someone at home.

BILLY EVANS

Billy is fifteen years old. He helps to care for his older brother, Joseph, who has **cerebral palsy**. Billy finds their regular trips for hospital appointments interesting. He also likes being so involved in Joseph's life. 'I got invited to Joseph's sixth form leavers' disco, which was nice as I got included in his social life and to see what he does when he's at school'.

He really likes 'meeting people who are also young carers and becoming friends with them.' There is a lot that is hard about Billy's role, but

'when I see Joseph being happy, it makes me HAPPY.'

POPPY KELEMEN

Thirteen-year-old Poppy has been helping to care for her twin brother, Jack, all their lives. Jack has **spina bifida** and **hydrocephalus**. These mean he sometimes needs support to get around and take care of himself. Jack has also spent a lot of time in hospital.

'I've learned lots of nursing skills and how to take care of Jack's medical needs. If things go wrong with his health, he comes to me. When I go to see him in hospital, I understand what the doctors and nurses are talking about. Mum and Dad trust me to do a lot of the caring.'

Like many twins, Poppy and Jack are very close and have a lot of fun together. 'When I do his nighttime dressings we have a race to see who gets to peel the satisfying square plaster. When we see each other at school, we nudge each other and laugh. Jack's always using his disability to get out of doing stuff like loading the dishwasher and doing the recycling, but Mum knows his tricks. Sometimes we both do trick her, though, and she lets us get away with things.'

It can be hard:

'Sometimes we have to take MORE TIME to do things. We need PATIENCE. Sometimes I have to help Jack with his physio or dressings when I want to be with my friends or am just tired.'

But Poppy loves 'seeing the amazing things Jack can do'. During the UK's lockdown in the 2020 COVID-19 pandemic, Jack joined many others completing the London Marathon from their own homes or local parks. Jack did five kilometres of the race on his wheelchair rollers in the garden, on a video link with a team of other young wheelchair users. 'We were all cheering him on from the top window!' Poppy says.

'Jack has to try so much harder than the rest of us. He usually moans about it but when he gets there it makes it worthwhile. I am really proud he is my brother. I think I feel differently – better – about life having a disabled brother to remind me what is important.'

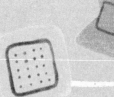

DEFINITIONS

CATHETERIZATION: the process of inserting a flexible tube into the body for removing fluid

CLINICAL PSYCHOLOGIST: a person qualified to assess and treat mental illness and behavioural problems

CPR: (short for cardiopulmonary resuscitation) a procedure for keeping the circulation of blood and oxygen in the body going by pumping the chest and breathing into the mouth and nose

GP: general practitioner, a doctor based in the community

CEREBRAL PALSY: a group of lifelong conditions that affect a person's ability to move

SPINA BIFIDA: when a baby's spine and spinal cord do not develop properly before birth, causing a gap

HYDROCEPHALUS: a build-up of fluid in the brain

PSYCHIATRIC: relating to mental illness or its treatment

HEALTH HEROES IN THE FIELD

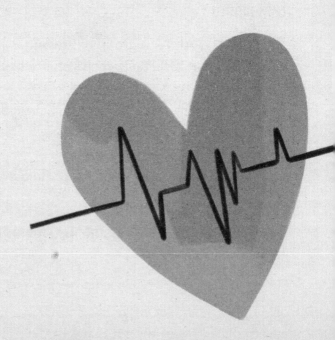

Most of the time nowadays, if we are receiving treatment or care for injury or illness, it will take place within a clean, controlled and relatively calm setting, such as a hospital, doctor's surgery or clinic. But health heroes are also working hard in places that are the exact opposite of this: in war zones, refugee camps or places in the world where people are poor or there is a lot of disease.

Throughout history, medical advances were often made or first tried out on battlefields. We have already seen how Florence Nightingale and Mary Seacole cared for wounded soldiers during the Crimean War, which resulted in nursing becoming a profession for the first time.

Here are some medical organizations that were set up to do incredible work around the world – and some of the health heroes who work for them!

INTERNATIONAL RED CROSS

Henry Dunant was a Swiss businessman who was horrified by the suffering of wounded soldiers he'd seen in war. In 1863 he set up a movement that would become the Red Cross and Red Crescent, to create societies of volunteers to provide kindness and help for those suffering during war, while remaining neutral.

Today, the movement is made up of 80 million people all around the world, working in a range of different ways – including treating and caring for the sick and wounded.

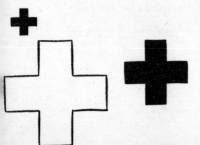

MÉDECINS SANS FRONTIÈRES

Sometimes known by the English translation of Doctors Without Borders, this is an international organization of medics working where people are at war, and in places affected by natural disasters and disease. It was created in 1971 by a group of French doctors and journalists who wanted to give people access to medical care wherever they were from and whatever their race, religion or political beliefs. In 1999, Médecins Sans Frontières won the Nobel Peace Prize (one of six awards given every year to people who 'best benefit mankind with their actions') for its work. Today, it has around 67,000 members, and works in over seventy countries around the world.

DAVID NOTT

David is a Welsh surgeon who works in London, and is also one of the many thousands of heroes who volunteer with organizations like Médicins Sans Frontières and the Red Cross in disaster and war zones. He and his wife, Elly, also train doctors and nurses in emergency surgery. They have trained more than 800 doctors, who have gone on to help 2 million patients.

That's a lot!

Every year David takes unpaid leave from his London work to give medical aid all over the world – in places including Bosnia, Afghanistan, Sierra Leone, Liberia, Ivory Coast, Chad, Sudan, Yemen, the Democratic Republic of Congo, Haiti, Iraq, Pakistan, Libya, Syria, Central African Republic, Gaza and Nepal.

David has been given many awards for his work and has been called the 'Indiana Jones of surgery'.

THE WORLD HEALTH ORGANIZATION (WHO)

The World Health Organization aims to improve the health of people all across the globe with things like vaccines and medical advice. It helps countries deal with health emergencies, such as the COVID-19 pandemic.

CHRISTOPHER LEE

Christopher is a doctor, but instead of treating individual patients, his work involves partnering with various organizations, including the WHO. He says: 'The unprecedented COVID-19 pandemic has tested the limits of all of the skills I have accumulated over my lifetime. I oversee a thirty-one-country project to train more than 20,000 African healthcare workers about caring for COVID-19 patients and taking care of themselves. And I advise African governments. Of course it's been challenging, but this is what I have been training for. I feel lucky that I can help.'

Chris loves 'seeing successes in some of the most difficult places. I spend about half of my life now in Nigeria, supporting the newly formed Nigeria Centre for Disease Control. It has bloomed into a major public health success – and I have worked with some of the most inspiring colleagues I have ever known! It's not easy to make change, but working with the right people, anything can be done.'

While qualifying as a doctor, Chris worked with homeless people in Boston, where he discovered that 'the experience of *homelessness itself* sickened people', then with locals after the 2004 tsunami in South East Asia and the 2010 earthquake in Haiti.

'By the time I finished my medical training in San Francisco, I wanted to do something "big". So I moved to New York and started working as an Epidemic Intelligence Service (EIS) officer. These are what the media calls "disease detectives".' This later led him to Guinea to assist ebola sufferers.

Chris works very hard and is away from home a lot but he says, 'the work and each small success make this worthwhile.'

CLAP FOR THE CARERS

There are so many more health heroes in the world than we have been able to meet in this book. Maybe you are related to one, or live next door to one – you almost certainly have some as your neighbours; some were probably there when you were born, and any time you or your family have needed medicine or vaccinations or help with your body or mind since. Perhaps one day you'll be a health hero too.

A thousand thank yous and all of the applause and banging of drums for the health, keyworker and other heroes who helped with or featured in this book:

Hassan Akkad; Alpha Barry; Abdullah Bashir; Lorna Begg; Brynn Bell; Roma Bissessar; Conor Broderick; Jason Campbell; Alexa Canardy; Sarah Clarke; Beth Cox;

Rebecca Crespi; Lucy Deacon; Shelby Delaney; Vicki Douglas; Sarah Dowd; Sarah Driver; Katherine Dryden; Rachel Elf; Billy Evans; Anna Fairley; Atul Gawande; Barbara George; Harry Josephine Giles; Taylor Harkness; Aileen Hickey; Shireen Hickey; Poppy Kelemen; Sarah Kelemen; Sally Kilner; Becky Lantzos; Christopher Lee; Gillian Lewis; Jamie Miles; Maggie May; Matt Morgan; Carly Murdoch; R. P. Narayan; Mia Noah; David Nott; Olamide Orekunrin; Jeremy Rogers; Yvonne Rogers; Susie Scott; Mohan Sekeram; Issy Sharratt; Pauline Sharratt; Ranjit Singh; Hannah Stevens; Nicola Stone; Sujith Subesinghe; Elizabeth Taylor; Hannah Warner; Helen Wilson; and everyone at All About Trans.

And for all health heroes everywhere.

LOVED **HEALTH HEROES**?

Here's more inspiring non-fiction from Simon & Schuster

Discover the gripping true story of

GRETA THUNBERG!

You're never too small to make a difference . . .

BE EMPOWERED BY THESE
INCREDIBLE PEOPLE
AND START CHANGING
THE WORLD NOW!

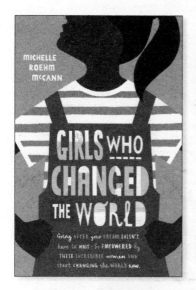

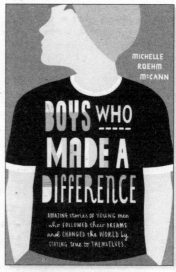

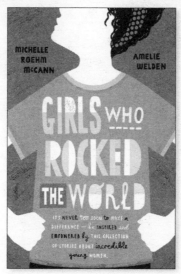

IT'S NOT JUST PEOPLE
WHO CHANGE THE WORLD!

Learn how geography has shaped our history . . .